Special Symbols:

This book is organized to guide the individual through the training. In addition to the Notes section there are a number of symbols used to help the participant throughout the presentation and workshop. For your convenience these symbols are repeated at the introduction of each section of this workbook.

Suggestion:

This symbol represents a suggestion or is a general statement relating to facilitation of the training

Tip:

This symbol represents a tip to the Facilitator and is specific to the concept that the Facilitator is presenting.

Question:

This symbol represents a question that may be asked to the Facilitator or to the participants in the workshop. It is intended to foster interaction during the training.

Table of Contents

Section 1

Section 2

Section 3

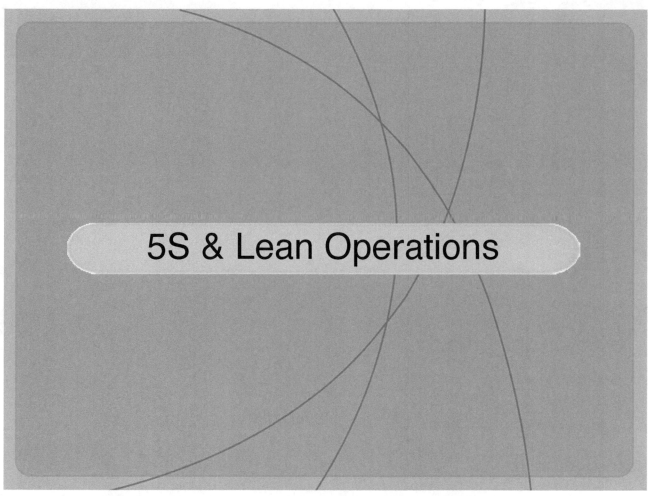

5S & Lean Operations

Participant Workbook

In this Section

- Learn the context of 5S
- Discover how 5S fits into improvement projects
- Study the 7 Wastes of Operations
- Content of the workshop

Participant Workbook Provided To:

_____

 Suggestion   **Tip**   **Question**

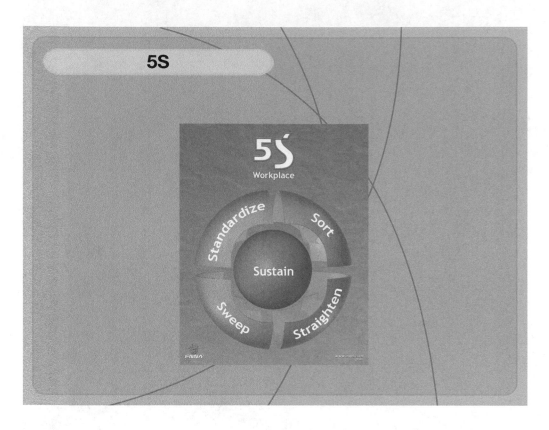

Notes, Slide 1:

_____

_____

_____

_____

_____

_____

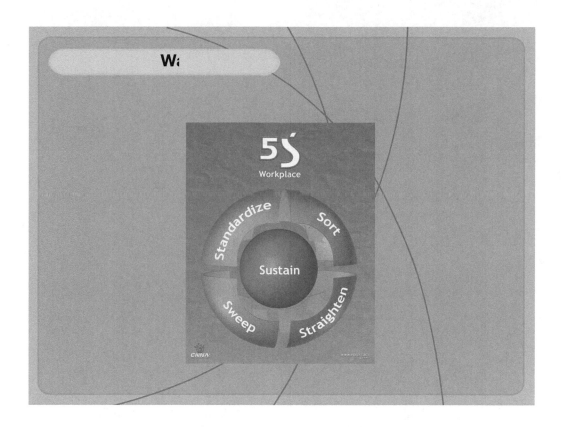

Notes, Slide 1 continued:

_____

_____

_____

_____

_____

_____

Tip:

Pay particular attention to the Facilitator when learning about a clean operation.

Question:

What do people generally think of an operation that is clean?

_____

_____

_____

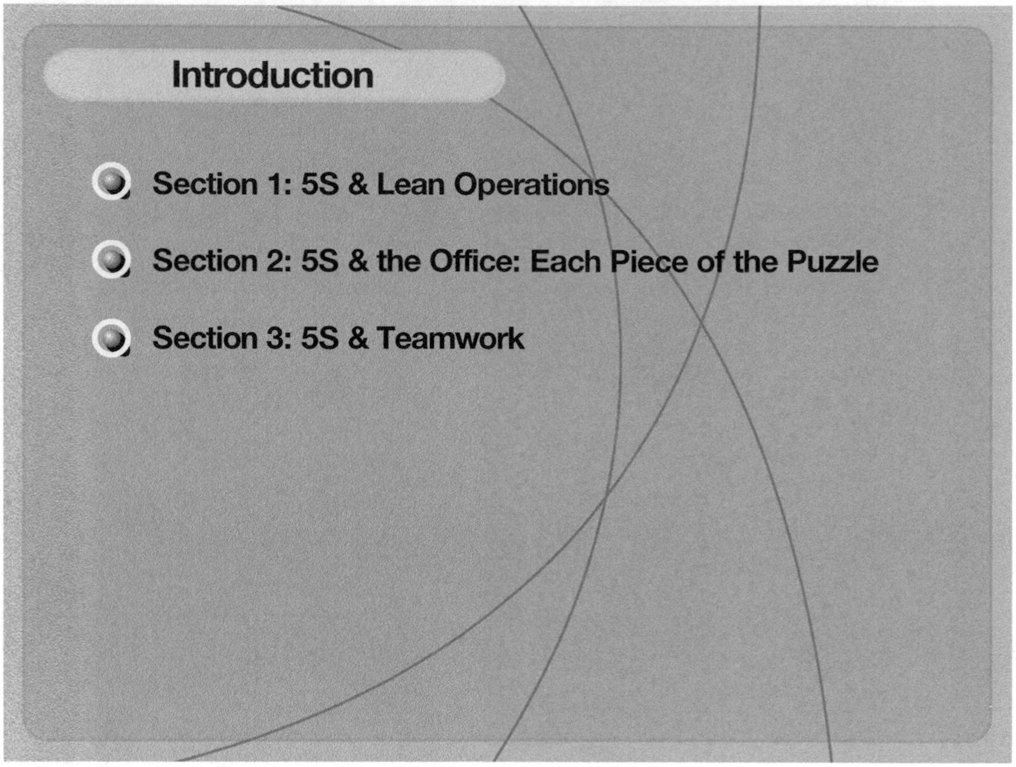

Introduction

- Section 1: 5S & Lean Operations

- Section 2: 5S & the Office: Each Piece of the Puzzle

- Section 3: 5S & Teamwork

Notes, Slide 2:

_____

_____

_____

_____

_____

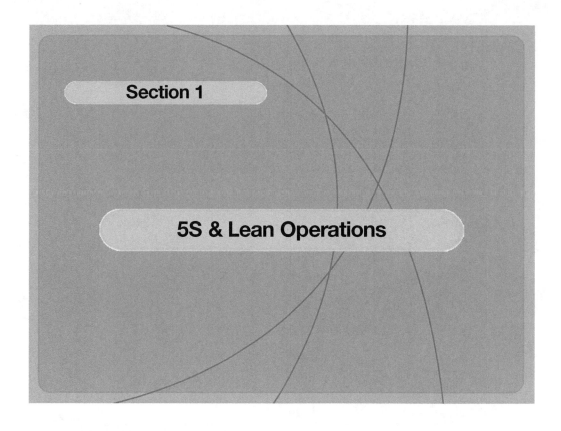

Section 1

5S & Lean Operations

Notes, Slide 3:

_____

_____

_____

_____

_____

_____

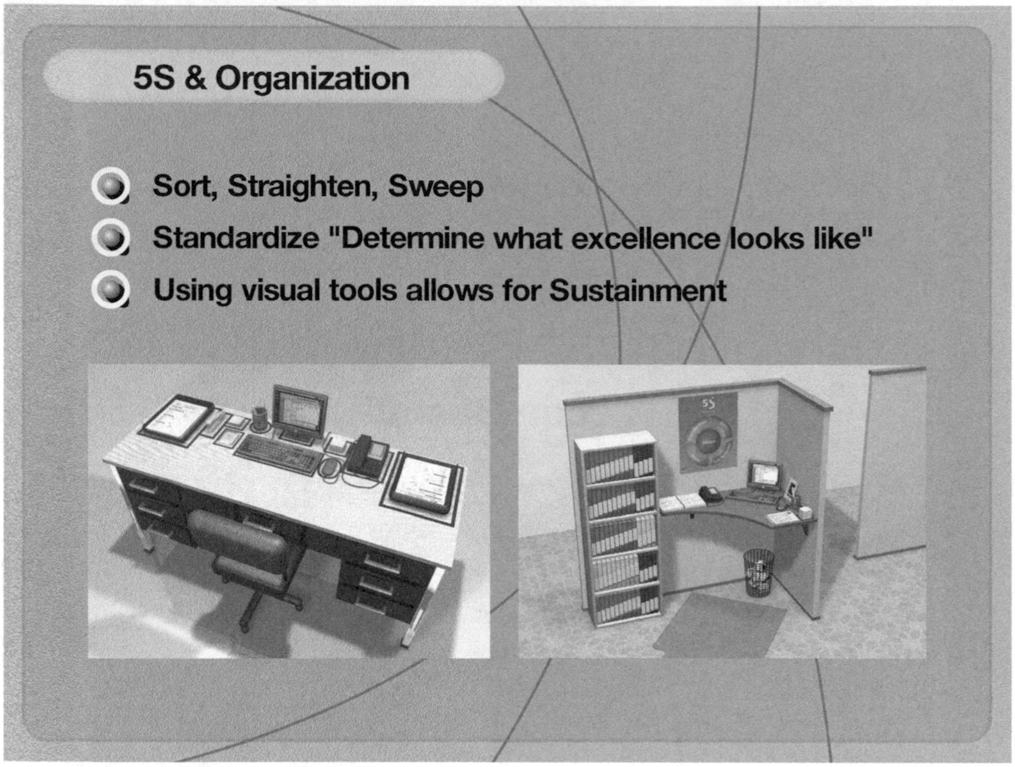

5S & Organization

- Sort, Straighten, Sweep
- Standardize "Determine what excellence looks like"
- Using visual tools allows for Sustainment

Notes, Slide 4:

_____

_____

_____

_____

_____

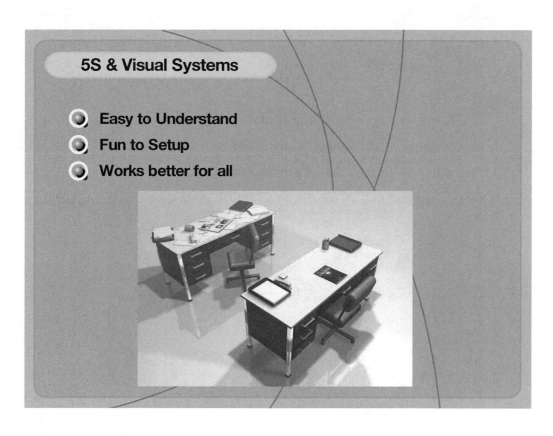

Notes, Slide 5:

_____

_____

_____

_____

_____

_____

Question:

Can you think of any kind of job that may require the need to be visual?

_____

_____

_____

Why 5S

- Allows us to maintain a more organized area
- Able to clean less and clean easier
- Makes our work area more productive

  - Makes the 7 Wastes obvious
  - Creates a standard for improvement
  - A way to get many people involved
  - Low real cost, high-impact for company

Notes, Slide 6:

_____

_____

_____

_____

_____

Question:

Why are we doing 5S?

_____

_____

_____

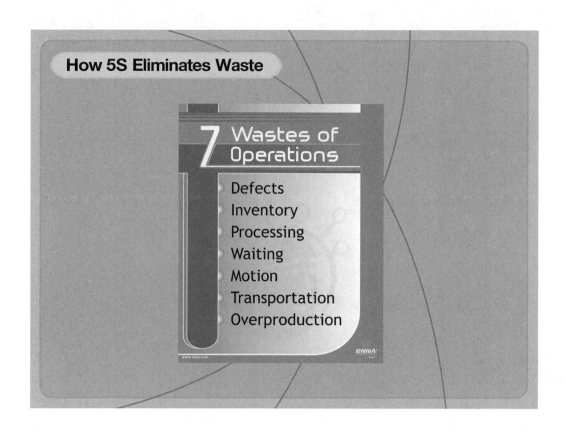

Notes, Slide 7:

Tip:
Focus on the 7 Wastes
and what the defini-
tions are.

_____

_____

_____

_____

_____

_____

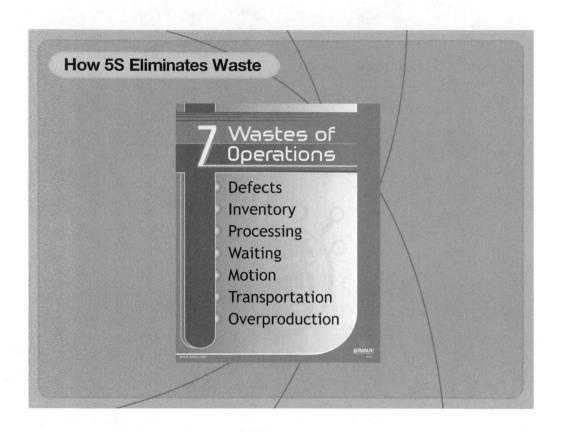

Notes, Slide 7 continued:

_____

_____

_____

_____

_____

_____

Tip:

The 7 Wastes are a fundamental building block of 5S. Ask the facilitator to fully explain the wastes so that you understand them completely.

Defects

Producing bad information, having extra information, wrong information, incomplete information, and/or having to redo work.

Possible Causes:

- Batch Processing
- Input Errors
- Questionable product design
- Poor work instructions

Notes, Slide 8:

_____

_____

_____

_____

Waste Definition: _____

_____

Additional Example: _____

_____

Inventory

Any material in the area other than what is immediately needed for the next process, stage, or step.

Possible Causes:

- Long processing times
- Supplier dependence
- Individual department design
- Just-in-case logic
- Unknown market demand

Notes, Slide 9:

_____

_____

_____

_____

Waste Definition: _____

_____

Additional Example: _____

_____

Question:

What are the three stages that inventory lives as in your company?

_____

_____

_____

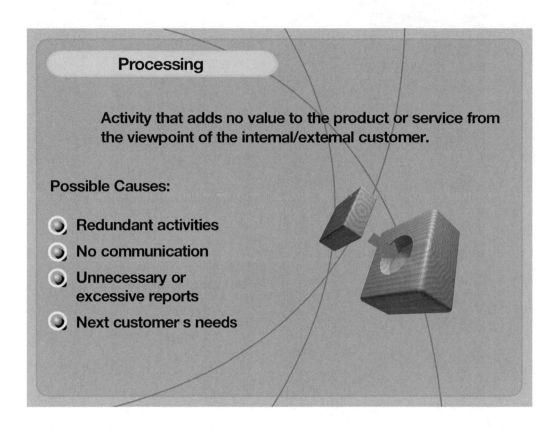

Processing

Activity that adds no value to the product or service from the viewpoint of the internal/external customer.

Possible Causes:

- Redundant activities
- No communication
- Unnecessary or excessive reports
- Next customer s needs

Notes, Slide 10:

_____

_____

_____

_____

Waste Definition: _____

_____

Additional Example: _____

_____

Tip:
This is the hardest waste to find. However, the solution is simple. If you think about it, if it is truly a waste of processing, then the ultimate solution is to find a way to not do it.

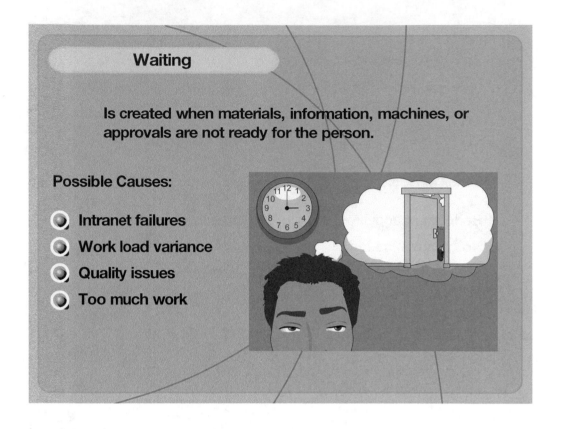

Waiting

Is created when materials, information, machines, or approvals are not ready for the person.

Possible Causes:

- Intranet failures
- Work load variance
- Quality issues
- Too much work

Notes, Slide 11:

_____

_____

_____

_____

Waste Definition: _____

_____

Additional Example: _____

_____

Tip:
Try purposely waiting rather than doing something. It is hard to wait.

Question:

What are some times that you have waited? What are you waiting for?

_____

_____

_____

Notes, Slide 12:

_____

_____

_____

_____

Waste Definition: _____

_____

Additional Example: _____

_____

Transportation

Moving information, paperwork, drawings, or ma[terial]
from one process to another process.

Possible Causes:

- Batch processing systems
- WIP storage for jobs
- Layout of the facility
- Job staging
- Utilization of office

Notes, Slide 13:

_____

_____

_____

_____

Waste Definition: _____

_____

Additional Example: _____

_____

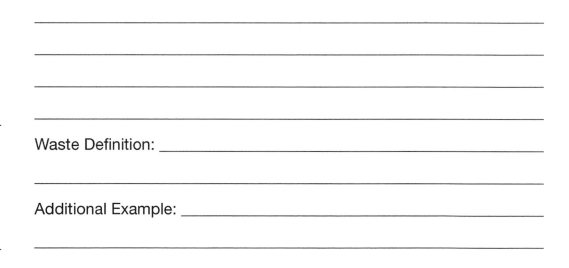

Overproduction

Making more components/products than the next process (or internal/external customer) requires.

Possible Causes:

- Just-in-case logic
- Focus on equipment only
- Setup times for processing jobs
- Keep-working environment
- Demand issues in each dept.

Notes, Slide 14:

_____

_____

_____

_____

Waste Definition: _____

_____

Additional Example: _____

_____

Tip:
Operations should look at ways to only produce what is truly needed. Anything more will result in loss of efficiency and effectiveness.

Question:

Why is overproduction so detrimental to an organization?

_____

_____

_____

5S & Lean Operations

Most, if not all, of the essential tools of Lean have the 5S as the key building blocks.

Examples:

- OEE
- 3P
- Design of Flow
- Lean Accounting
- Office Kaizen

Notes, Slide 15:

_____

_____

_____

_____

_____

_____

5S & Organization:
Each Piece of the Puzzle

Participant Workbook

In this Section

- The meaning behind 5S
- Applying 5S in your area and environment
- The five elements of 5S
- Guide for participants through the proper sequence of learning 5S

 Suggestion   **Tip**   **Question**

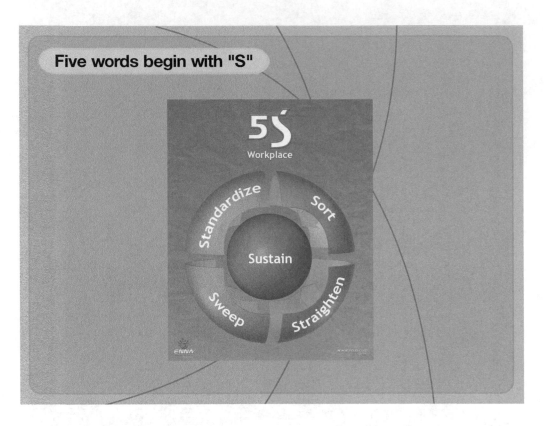

Five words begin with "S"

Notes, Slide 17:

_____

_____

_____

_____

_____

_____

Question:

How many S's were there originally and which company founded the term?

_____

_____

_____

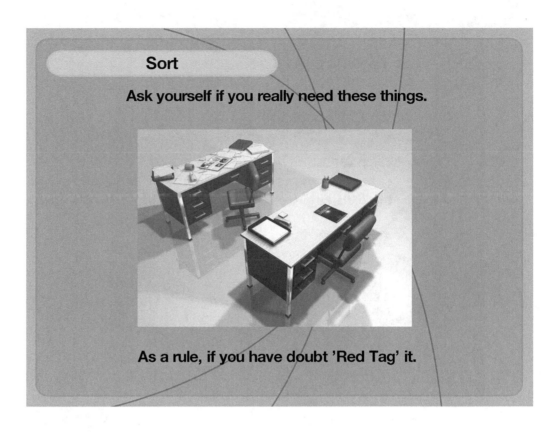

Sort

Ask yourself if you really need these things.

As a rule, if you have doubt 'Red Tag' it.

Notes, Slide 18:

_____

_____

_____

_____

Tip:
When sorting, make
two categories:
1) what is needed for
the job, and
2) everything else.

Sort Action Defined: _____

_____

Additional Example: _____

_____

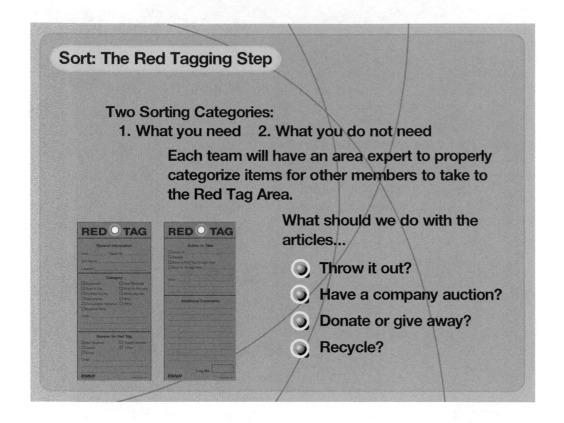

Notes, Slide 19:

_____

_____

_____

_____

_____

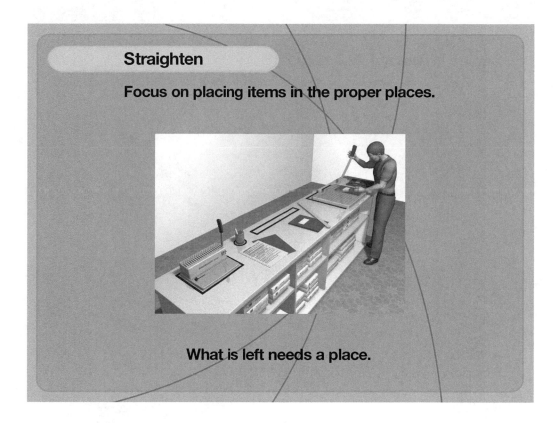

Notes, Slide 20:

_____

_____

_____

_____

Straighten Action Defined: _____

_____

Additional Example: _____

_____

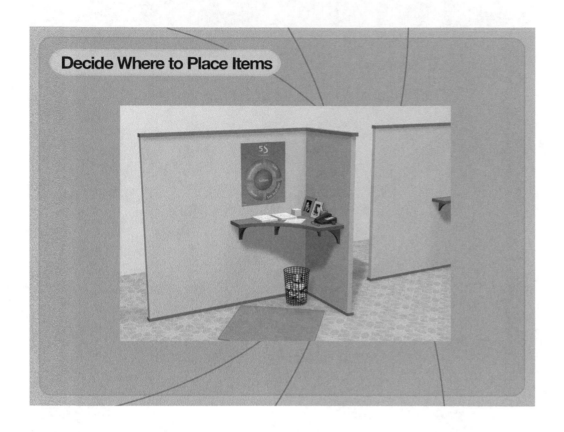

Decide Where to Place Items

Notes, Slide 21:

Tip:

Look at the above illustration. What workstation solutions can you find that minimize the waste of motion?

Example of Straighten

- Why do office supply stores position items on shelves the way they do?

- Can this apply to what we do?

Notes, Slide 22:

_____

_____

_____

_____

_____

_____

Tip:
Try to reach for anything in your work area. The goal of Straighten is to eliminate reaching.

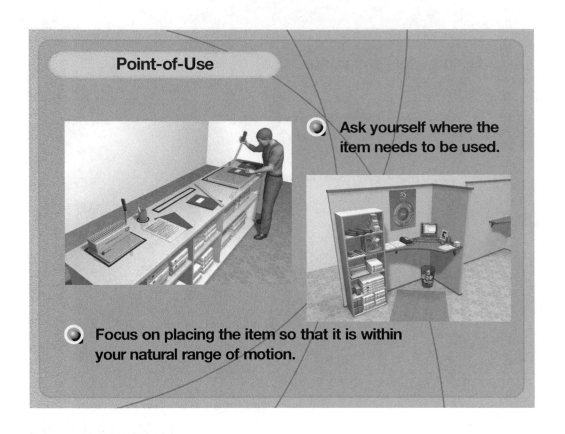

Notes, Slide 23:

_____

_____

_____

_____

_____

_____

Items Have Homes

Are these illustrations good examples of Straighten?

Notes, Slide 24:

_____

_____

_____

_____

_____

_____

Tip:
Use Straighten to get working, rather than just preparing to work.

Notes, Slide 25:

_____

_____

_____

_____

_____

_____

Sweep

- Clean enough to identify root problem
- Move beyond just having a clean area
- Clean to discover how not to clean

Notes, Slide 26:

_____

_____

_____

_____

Tip:
Remember, we are cleaning to...

Sweep Action Defined: _____

_____

Additional Example: _____

_____

Question:

Why are we cleaning during this workshop?

_____

_____

_____

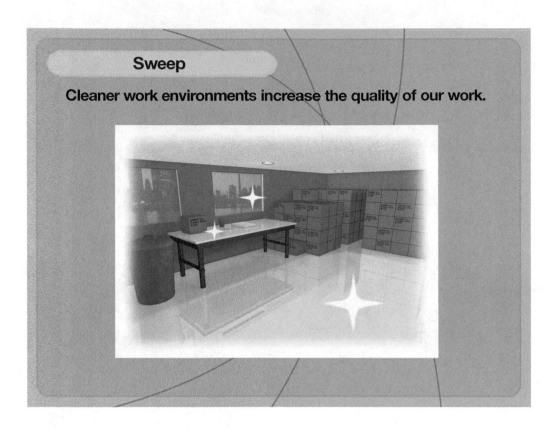

Sweep

Cleaner work environments increase the quality of our work.

Notes, Slide 27:

_____

_____

_____

_____

_____

_____

Tip:
Combining ideas together will find solutions to reducing and even eliminating the need for sweeping.

Standardize

Ask yourself how to create a work area free of checklists.

Once you see it, you know what needs to be done even without years of experience.

Notes, Slide 28:

_____

_____

_____

_____

_____

_____

Question:

Can you think of an example of good standardization?

_____

_____

_____

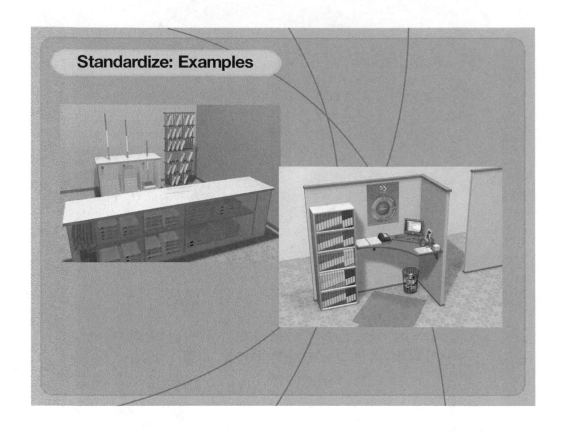

Standardize: Examples

Notes, Slide 29:

_____

_____

_____

_____

Standardize Action Defined: _____

_____

Additional Example: _____

_____

Tip:
When creating a standard, incorporate symbols, colors, and/or physical characteristics.

5S Sustainment Schedule

Start Date: _____   Work Area:_____

Person Responsible	Specific Location	Frequency of Activity	Activities to Perform

Notes, Slide 30:

_____

_____

_____

_____

_____

_____

Question:

Why is it useful to employ the 5S Sustainment Schedule?

_____

_____

_____

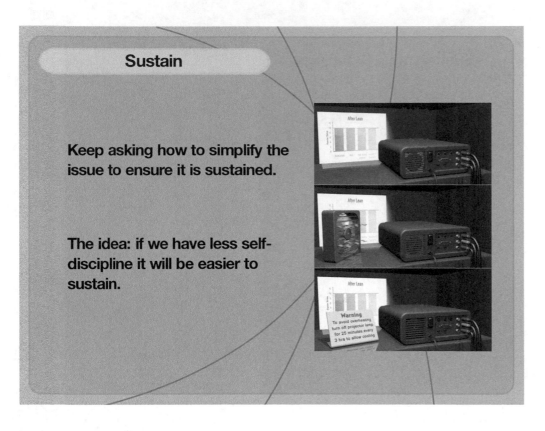

Notes, Slide 31:

_____

_____

_____

_____

_____

_____

Question:

What is the ultimate goal of 5S?

_____

_____

_____

Sustain

- Management shows commitment to program
- Everyone leads by being an example of 5S
- 5S is a component of every workshop
- Goal is to have customers tour your facility
- Use the Evaluating 5S Forms to assess 5S score

Notes, Slide 32:

_____

_____

_____

_____

Sustain Action Defined: _____

_____

Additional Example: _____

_____

Tip:

Use your past employment experience to help develop sustaining changes. Often past examples help develop solutions. Pull examples from the past and see how the team can use them.

5S Sustainment Schedule

5S Sustainment Schedule

Start Date: _April 08, 2008_   Work Area: _Order Entry_

Person Responsible	Specific Location	Frequency of Activity	Activities to Perform
Sarah Janzen	Order Entry - Desk 3	weekly	Organize & clean area, turn off HVAC before leaving.

© ENNA   www.enna.com

Notes, Slide 33:

_____

_____

_____

_____

_____

_____

Long-Term 5S Success

- Management is expected to be involved in activities
- Involvement of everyone
- 7 Wastes are an integral part of 5S
- Link improvement to a financial benefit

Notes, Slide 34:

_____

_____

_____

_____

_____

_____

Question:

5S needs the commitment of who?

_____

_____

_____

Review & Summary

- What are the 5S words?

- Which S is the most important?

- Can you relate to the need for 5S?

- What are the 7 Wastes?

- What is your responsibility?

Notes, Slide 35:

_____

_____

_____

_____

Final thoughts on this section: _____

_____

_____

Tip:
Write down the answers
to these questions to
summarize this section.

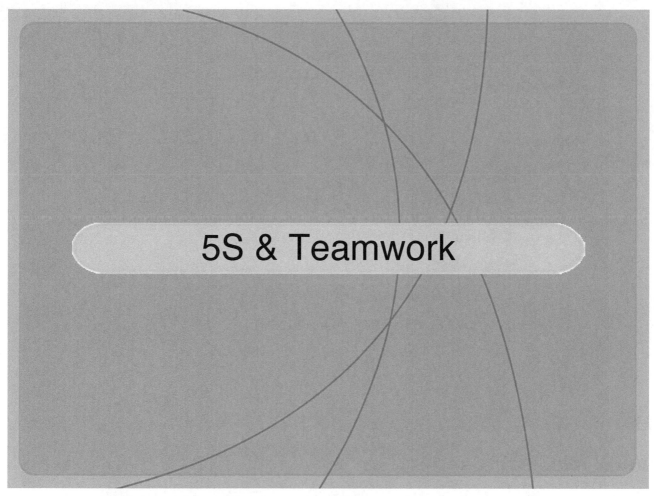

5S & Teamwork

Participant Workbook

In this Section

Now that we have gained some knowledge we are going to put it into practice.

– Learn the 5S Evaluation process
– Learn the 30 Day Action Log
– Learn the 5S Sustainment Schedule
– Discuss the workshop format

 Suggestion   **Tip**   **Question**

5S Teamwork

Steps:

1: 5S Evaluation

2: Sort- Red Tag Activity

3: Straighten- Point of Use Storage

4: Sweep- Clean Area

5: Standardize- Visual Management

6: Sustain- Refine and Schedule

Notes, Slide 37:

_____

_____

_____

_____

_____

_____

5S Team

1. Evaluating 5S Team (2-3 people)

2. Photography Team (2 people)
   - Take pictures of the current state
   - Highlight key objects and areas

3. 5S Mapping Team (2-3 people)
   - Layout where people, materials, and equipment should be located (bird s eye view)

Notes, Slide 38:

_____

_____

Team Assigned To: _____

_____

Team Members Names: _____

_____

_____

Assigned Work Area:

_____

Additional Information: _____

_____

_____

Tip:
You will change roles as you move from assessment through to making changes, but your team should stay together.

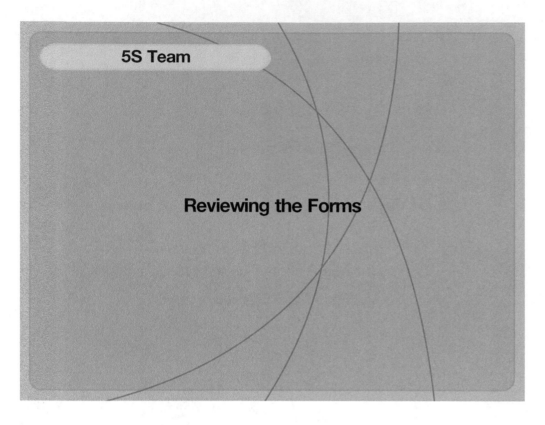

Notes, Slide 39:

_____

_____

_____

_____

_____

_____

5S Map

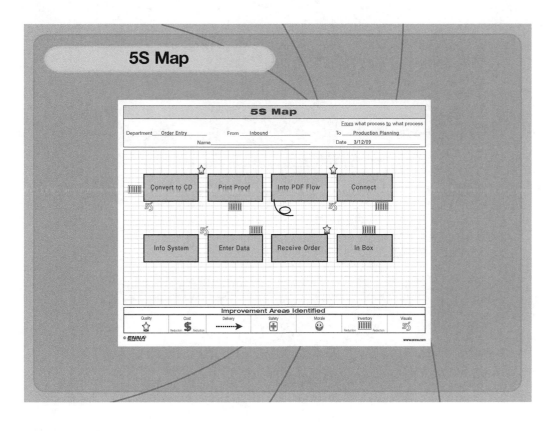

Notes, Slide 40:

_____

_____

_____

_____

_____

_____

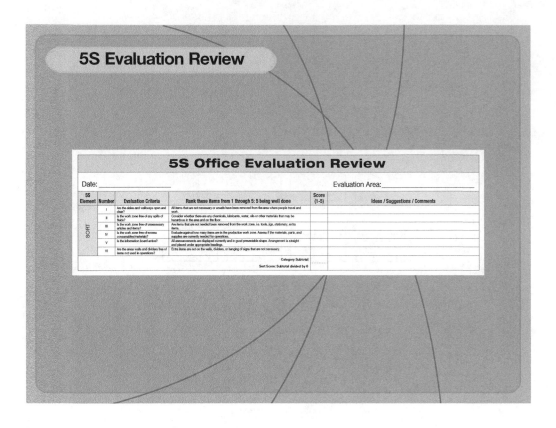

5S Evaluation Review

5S Office Evaluation Review

Date: _____ Evaluation Area: _____

5S Element	Number	Evaluation Criteria	Rank these items from 1 through 5; 5 being well done	Score (1-5)	Ideas / Suggestions / Comments
SORT	I	Are the aisles and walkways open and clear?	All items that are not necessary or unsafe have been removed from the area where people travel and work.		
	II	Is the work zone free of any spills of fluids?	Consider whether there are any chemicals, lubricants, water, oils or other materials that may be hazardous in the area and on the floor.		
	III	Is the work zone free of unnecessary articles and items?	Are items that are not needed been removed from the work zone, i.e. tools, jigs, stationary, extra items.		
	IV	Is the work zone free of excess consumables/materials?	Evaluate against how many items are in the production work zone. Assess if the materials, parts, and supplies are currently needed for operations.		
	V	Is the information board active?	All announcements are displayed currently and in good presentable shape. Arrangement is straight and placed under appropriate headings.		
	VI	Are the areas walls and dividers free of items not used in operations?	Extra items are not on the walls, dividers, or hanging of signs that are not necessary.		
			Category Subtotal		
			Sort Score: Subtotal divided by 6		

Notes, Slide 41:

_____

_____

_____

_____

_____

Tip:
Be critical when evaluating the area; the initial evaluation serves as a baseline for further comparison.

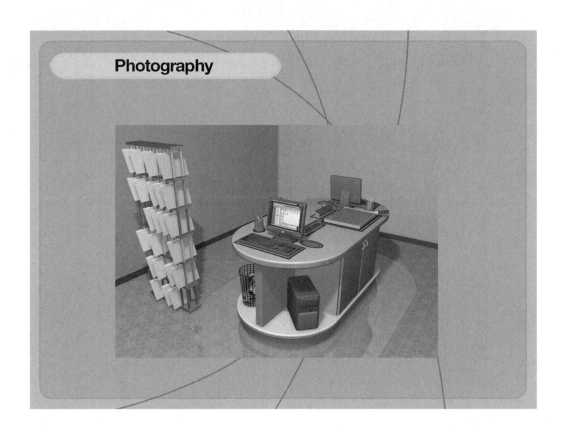

Notes, Slide 42:

_____

_____

_____

_____

_____

_____

Tip:

Lighting is key for photographs. Have the team borrow lights to make the items in the pictures really stand out.

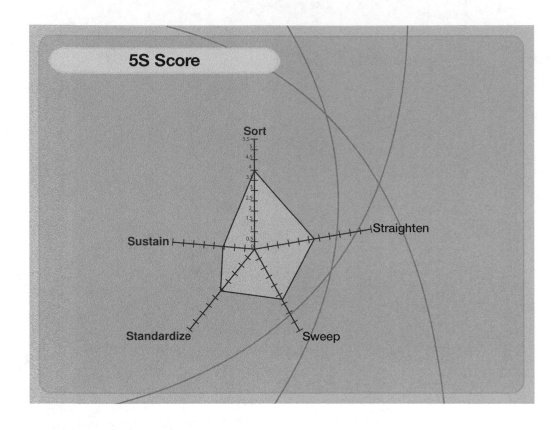

Notes, Slide 43:

_____

_____

_____

_____

_____

Tip:
We should be ready to
evaluate our current
state.

Red Tags/Red Tag Register

Red Tag Register

Project Date: _April 7-11, 2008_   Work Area: _Order Entry_

Item Description	Date Sorted	Log Number	Reason for Tag	Classification (i.e. need approval, other dept. needs to assess, throw out, etc.)
Spare File Folders	4/2/08	B001	Not needed at desk.	No need for approval.
Assorted Items	4/3/08	B002	Too much stuff in area.	Need approval of management.
Extra Printer	4/4/08	B003	In work area but not used.	Need product development approval.
Print Drums	4/4/08	B004	Not needed in area - should be stored elsewhere.	Back to stores, not Red Tag Area.

Notes, Slide 44 & 45:

Tip:
If you have any doubt, Red Tag it and "throw it out" of the area.

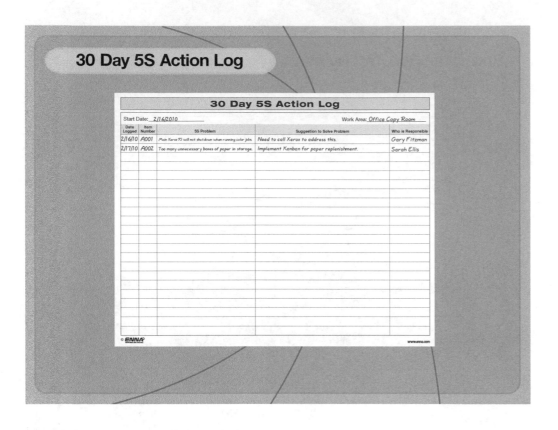

30 Day 5S Action Log

Start Date: 2/16/2010 **Work Area:** Office Copy Room

Date Logged	Item Number	5S Problem	Suggestion to Solve Problem	Who is Responsible
2/16/10	A001	Main Xerox 95 will not shutdown when running color jobs.	Need to call Xerox to address this.	Gary Fitzman
2/17/10	A002	Too many unnecessary boxes of paper in storage.	Implement Kanban for paper replenishment.	Sarah Ellis

© ENNA www.enna.com

Notes, Slide 46:

_____

_____

_____

_____

_____

_____

Tip:

Only place items on the 30 Day 5S Action Log that the team has agreed is an item for that list. Your team should all agree before adding an item to the 30 Day 5S Action Log. You may have to get support from other departments.

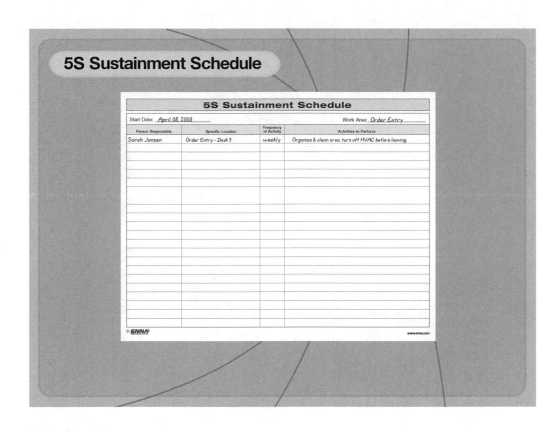

Notes, Slide 47:

_____

_____

_____

_____

_____

_____

Tip:
Team members are expected to commit to 5S by providing innovative ways to solve problems.

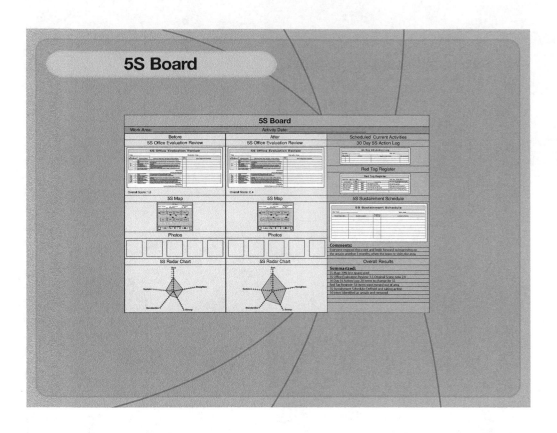

Notes, Slide 48:

_____

_____

_____

_____

_____

_____

5S Assessment

Facilitator: _____   Name: _____

Workshop: _____   Date: _____

Circle or write the answer that best fits the question or completes the statement.

1. _____ 5S originally had _____ S's.
   a) 4
   b) 1
   c) 2

2. _____ What company started what is now known as 5S?
   a) Volvo
   b) Toyota
   c) Ford

3. _____ What is the first S of the 5S's?
   a) Straighten
   b) Sort
   c) Sweep

4. _____ of the 7 Wastes of Operations which one is the worst?
   a) Overproduction
   b) Inventory
   c) Defects

5. _____ If a company implements 5S successfully, the need for self-discipline is _____.
   a) Eliminated
   b) Reduced
   c) Increased

6. _____ 5S is one of the building blocks of _____?
   a) Operations
   b) Cleanliness
   c) Lean

7. _____ Why do we clean during 5S?
   a) To inspect
   b) Because it is the right thing to do
   c) To prevent bad parts

8. _____ What does inventory exist in the company as?
   a) Raw, WIP, FG
   b) GF, WIP, RAW
   c) PIW, WAR, FG

9. _____ The S in Straighten allows for a person to have minimal _____.
   a) Work
   b) Waiting
   c) Motion

10. _____ What is the 5S Sustainment Schedule used for?
    a) Recording workshop activity
    b) Recording the cleaning that is needed
    c) Scheduling the next workshop

11. _____ For 5S to be successful we need the involvement of _____ .
    a) Top management
    b) Entire department
    c) Everyone

12. _____ The 5S Map provides a simple _____ point of view of the work area.
    a) Bird's eye
    b) Planning
    c) Outline

13. _____ Processing is the hardest waste to find because _____ .
    a) There are so many processes
    b) It may initially seem to be a value-added step
    c) It is totally necessary

14. _____ The 30-Day Action Log allows the company to _____.
    a) Document a list of unsolvable problems
    b) List workshop problems to be solved on one document
    c) Demonstrate its commitment to 5S

1:c, 2:b, 3:b, 4:a, 5:b, 6:c, 7:a, 8:a, 9:c, 10:b, 11:c, 12:a, 13:b, 14:b

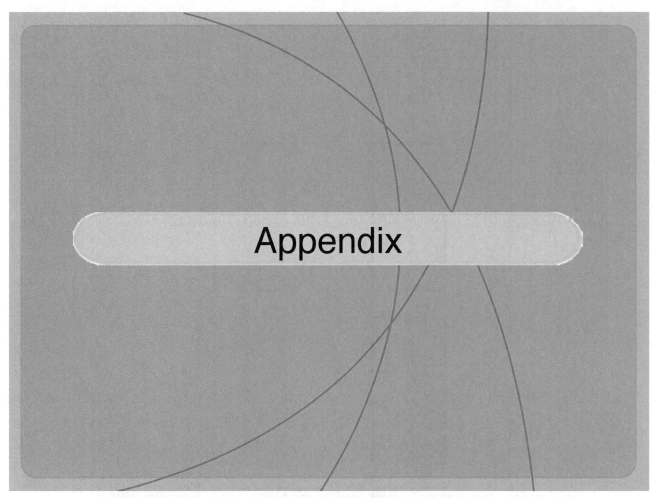

Participant Workbook

In this Section

You will find copies of the forms used in the workshop filled out for your reference.

5S Map

Department ___Order Entry___ From ___Inbound___

Name___

From what process to what process

To ___Production Planning___

Date ___3/12/09___

Convert to CD

Print Proof

Into PDF Flow

Connect

Info System

Enter Data

Receive Order

In Box

Improvement Areas Identified

Quality	Cost	Delivery	Safety	Morale	Inventory	Visuals
	Reduction				Reduction	Reduction
	Reduction				Reduction	

5S Office Evaluation Review

Date: _____

Evaluation Area: _____

5S Element	Number	Evaluation Criteria	Rank these items from 1 through 5: 5 being well done	Score (1-5)	Ideas / Suggestions / Comments
SORT	I	Are the aisles and walkways open and clear?	All items that are not necessary or unsafe have been removed from the area where people travel and work.		
	II	Is the work zone free of any spills of fluids?	Consider whether there are any chemicals, lubricants, water, oils or other materials that may be hazardous in the area and on the floor.		
	III	Is the work zone free of unnecessary articles and items?	Are items that are not needed been removed from the work zone, i.e. tools, jigs, stationary, extra items.		
	IV	Is the work zone free of excess consumables/materials?	Evaluate against how many items are in the production work zone. Assess if the materials, parts, and supplies are currently needed for operations.		
	V	Is the information board active?	All announcements are displayed currently and in good presentable shape. Arrangement is straight and placed under appropriate headings.		
	VI	Are the areas walls and dividers free of items not used in operations?	Extra items are not on the walls, dividers, or hanging of signs that are not necessary.		

Category Subtotal

Sort Score: Subtotal divided by 6

Red Tag Register

Work Area: _Order Entry_

Project Date: _April 7-11, 2008_

Item Description	Date Sorted	Log Number	Reason for Tag	Classification (i.e. need approval, other dept. needs to assess, throw out, etc.)
Spare File Folders	4/2/08	B001	Not needed at desk.	No need for approval.
Assorted Items	4/3/08	B002	Too much stuff in area.	Need approval of management.
Extra Printer	4/4/08	B003	In work area but not used.	Need product development approval.
Print Drums	4/4/08	B004	Not needed in area - should be stored elsewhere.	Back to stores, not Red Tag Area.

30 Day 5S Action Log

Start Date: ___2/16/2010___

Work Area: ___Office Copy Room___

Date Logged	Item Number	5S Problem	Suggestion to Solve Problem	Who is Responsible
2/16/10	A001	Main Xerox 95 will not shutdown when running color jobs.	Need to call Xerox to address this.	Gary Fitzman
2/17/10	A002	Too many unnecessary boxes of paper in storage.	Implement Kanban for paper replenishment.	Sarah Ellis

5S Sustainment Schedule

Start Date: _April 08, 2008_

Work Area: _Order Entry_

Person Responsible	Specific Location	Frequency of Activity	Activities to Perform
Sarah Janzen	Order Entry - Desk 3	weekly	Organize & clean area, turn off HVAC before leaving.

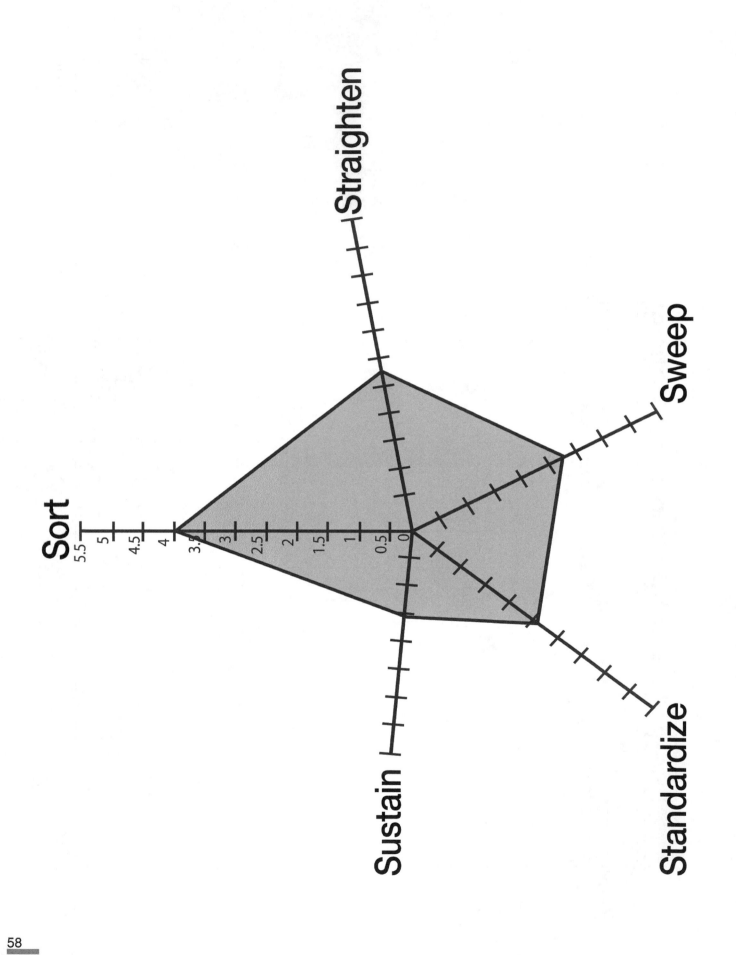